THE
ORCHESTRA

CLASSIC *f*M
HANDY
GUIDES

THE
ORCHESTRA

DARREN HENLEY

First published 2015 by
Elliott and Thompson Limited
27 John Street
London WC1N 2BX
www.eandtbooks.com

ISBN: 978-1-90965-362-7

9 8 7 6 5 4 3 2 1

A catalogue record for this book is available from the
British Library.

Typesetting: Marie Doherty
Printed in the UK by TJ International Ltd

Contents

Introduction

At Classic FM, we spend a lot of our time dreaming up wonderful ways of making sure that as many people as possible across the UK have the opportunity to listen to classical music. As the nation's biggest classical music radio station, we feel that we have a responsibility to share the world's greatest music as widely as we can.

Over the years, we have written a variety of classical music books in all sorts of shapes and sizes. But we have never put together a series of books quite like this.

This set of books covers a whole range of aspects of classical music. They are all written in Classic FM's friendly, accessible style and you can rest assured that they are packed full of facts about classical music. Read separately, each book gives you a handy snapshot of a particular subject area. Added together, the series combines to offer a more detailed insight into the full story of classical music. Along the way, we shall be paying particular attention to some of the key composers whose music we play most often on the radio station, as well as examining many of classical music's subgenres.

These books are relatively small in size, so they are not going to be encyclopedic in their level of detail; there are other books out there that do that much better than we could ever hope to. Instead, they are intended to be enjoyable introductory guides that will be particularly useful to listeners who are beginning their voyage of discovery through the rich and exciting world of classical music. Drawing on the research we have undertaken for many of our previous Classic FM books, they concentrate on information rather than theory because we want to make this series of books attractive and inviting to readers who are not necessarily familiar with the more complex aspects of musicology.

For more information on this series, take a look at our website: www.ClassicFM.com/handyguides.

Preface

The great British conductor Sir Thomas Beecham left behind him a collection of witticisms on virtually every aspect of classical music life. As someone who spent his days – and nights – standing baton in hand in front of various groups of musicians, he developed a pretty acute understanding of what was required from them. 'There are two golden rules for an orchestra', he once said. 'Start together and finish together. The audience doesn't give a damn what goes on in between.'

Other conductors have offered a slightly more nuanced view on the role of the orchestra, but many of them recognise the power of the collective body of musicians that sat before them. Kurt Masur believed that 'You have to change your mind with every orchestra because every orchestra has a different character.' While composer and conductor Robert Schumann talked of the almost military might of a group of musicians playing together in unison, saying: 'I feel so entirely in my element with a full orchestra; even if my mortal enemies were marshalled before me, I could lead them, master them, surround them, or repulse them.'

There is no getting away from the importance of the orchestra in classical music. While works for solo instruments or small groups of musicians are without question a vital part of the lifeblood of the genre, there is nothing quite so special as hearing a performance by an orchestra at the top of its game. And, over the years, our greatest composers have proven this by marshalling the forces of countless orchestral musicians in the creation of many of the most enduring and popular classical works of all time.

one

Back at the Beginning

Originally the word 'orchestra' did not mean a group of people playing music at all. Instead, it was the place where they stood or sat. In a Greek amphitheatre, the natural slope of the seats was called the 'loilon'; the backdrop to the stage was known as the 'scena', and the semi-circular piece of flat ground between the two was the 'orchestra'. Eventually, it came to mean the people who played there, too.

The modern orchestra, like the ancient one before it, was also born in the theatre, where it accompanied plays and operas. The Dresden Staatskapelle is the world's oldest orchestra, tracing its roots back as far as 1548. It was soon joined by others, as churches, courts, cities and towns across

Europe founded their own ensembles over the following couple of centuries. The virtuoso Mannheim orchestra (run by the local Elector) was particularly important in advancing the cause. The UK's oldest surviving symphony orchestra is the Royal Liverpool Philharmonic Orchestra, which was founded in 1840 and became a fully professional band in 1853.

Orchestration

Orchestration is the part of a composer's job that sorts out who plays what. Usually it comes after the initial composing itself, once the central ideas have been created. Many composers consider it a completely separate procedure, and some are thought of as being greater masters of the process than others. Maurice Ravel, Hector Berlioz and Paul Dukas, for example, are all considered experts in the field.

Nikolai Rimsky-Korsakov was another such expert, making a habit of superbly orchestrating virtually everything that he laid his hands on. He was already strong in the area of orchestration while he was still at college, writing musical arrangements for the student band. He perfected his craft while he was in the navy, when he made a point of learning how to play just about every instrument of the orchestra.

Richard Wagner is worthy of a mention at the start of this book, too. When he could not get quite the right combination of orchestral colours to do justice to the sound that was in his head, he simply invented his own instrument to create it. The 'Wagner tuba' was the result. It is, in fact, more of a big horn than a tuba. Wagner employed it to great musical effect in his mammoth four-opera cycle, *The Ring*.

The Make-Up of the Orchestra

The biggest section of the orchestra is made up of string instruments. In a standard-sized symphony orchestra, you might find around thirty violins, a dozen or so violas, maybe ten cellos and around eight double-basses. That is a total of around sixty or so players in all – roughly two-thirds of the band. The reason that these numbers are not exact is that different composers call for slightly different musical configurations for each of their works, and in some repertoires conductors and managers can exercise a degree of choice.

The brass section typically comprises three trumpets, three trombones, four French horns and a tuba – allowing the composer to paint musical pictures with three high, four middle, three low and one very low brush. The brass section is undoubtedly loud: these eleven players alone can often drown out the entire string section because of the sheer volume of sound that their instruments are capable of producing.

Next are the woodwind instruments, which these days are not necessarily made of wood. This section is made up of two or three flutes, often a piccolo, a couple of oboes, four clarinets and perhaps a bass clarinet, two bassoons and possibly a contra-bassoon.

The final part of the orchestra is a percussion section of three or four players, playing various instruments, such as timpani, cymbals, side drums, bass drums, xylophones and triangles.

One or sometimes two harpists and a pianist, who might play the celesta when required, more or less complete the complement of a full standard symphony orchestra.

A chamber orchestra operates in a similar way to a symphony orchestra, but on a smaller scale, usually having a total of only around thirty play-ers on stage. Again, the exact range of instruments that turns up on the night will be dependent on the demands of the composer's score, but each of the sections of a chamber orchestra will have fewer musicians than its symphonic big brother.

two

The Conductor

Before we move on to look at the individual instruments of the orchestra, let's pause to examine the man or woman who makes absolutely no noise in an orchestral concert – but who demands the attention of both the audience and the players.

Conductors are the gods and goddesses of the classical music world. At the highest levels, they command hefty fees (unlike the rank-and-file performers they conduct) and can tell you what they will be doing sometimes many years into the future, so great are the demands on their musical time.

Their role, musically speaking, is not just the obvious one of using their baton or hands to keep time for all the players and/or singers in front of them to see. Conductors also play an important part as the channel for the overall interpretation of the music; they have a lot of say over how an orchestra makes a particular piece of music sound.

Some conductors choose to try to interpret a composer's wishes to the tiniest degree, hoping to bring out every nuance in the music as its writer intended it. Others prefer simply to be a channel for their own unique vision (perhaps audition would be a better word in this case) of the way the music should sound. Often this is done not just by means of time and dynamic, but via something wholly more indefinable: the quality of the conductor's presence on the podium; the rapport already established with the musicians; and even mere movements and gestures of the eyes.

Historically, conductors have not always been as they are today. Early on, a mixture of the keyboard player and the leader (the head of the first violins) would jointly keep the orchestra in line. In Jean-Baptiste Lully's day, in the 1600s, a conductor would thump the floor with a broom-sized stick in order to keep time, a practice that famously led to his death from gangrene when he hit his foot during a performance of his *Te Deum*.

Later, the composer Louis Spohr was just one of those at the forefront of refining conducting into what it is now, championing not only the use of the baton but also the addition of letters of the alphabet to scores, thus dividing them into navigable sections. The notion of conductors as musical interpreters originated in the nineteenth century, when changing attitudes to musical performance gave them far greater importance. Indeed, in many respects, composers such as Gustav Mahler and Richard Wagner were thought of in their day as conductors first and composers second.

Great conductors of the past have included Arturo Toscanini, Bruno Walter, Sir Thomas Beecham, Leopold Stokowski, Wilhelm Furtwängler, Sir Malcolm Sargent, Sir John Barbirolli, Sir Adrian Boult, Herbert von Karajan, Sir Charles Mackerras and Sir Colin Davis.

Today's great conductors include:

Marin Alsop

One of the few very successful female conductors, American-born Marin Alsop made her name in the UK first as the Principal Guest Conductor of the Royal Scottish National Orchestra and of the City of London Sinfonia and, subsequently, as the Principal Conductor of Bournemouth Symphony Orchestra. She is now Music Director of the Baltimore Symphony Orchestra and Principal Conductor of the São Paulo State Symphony Orchestra.

Riccardo Chailly

This Italian conductor made his name first as an opera conductor, before turning his expert attention to symphonic repertoire. Chailly's roles have included Principal Conductor of the Berlin Radio Symphony Orchestra, Principal Guest Conductor of the London Philharmonic Orchestra, Chief Conductor of the Royal Concertgebouw Orchestra, Chief Conductor of the Leipzig Gewandhaus Orchestra and Music Director of the Orchestra Sinfonica di Milano Giuseppe Verdi (known as La Verdi). The Principal Conductor of La Scala Milan as of January 2015, he will then take over there as Music Director in 2017. He has an exclusive recording contract with the Decca label, which has seen him produce a raft of critically acclaimed albums.

Gustavo Dudamel

One of the darlings of the classical music world, this global sensation came to public attention as the Music Director of the Simón Bolívar Symphony Orchestra, which is based in his native Venezuela. Dudamel now has the same role at the Los Angeles Philharmonic and also appears alongside many of the world's biggest orchestras as a guest conductor.

Valery Gergiev

Among the world's busiest conductors, Gergiev's roles include General Director of the Mariinsky Theatre, Principal Conductor of the London Symphony Orchestra, Music Director of the Munich Philharmonic and Artistic Director of the White Nights Festival in St Petersburg. His repertoire in both the recording studio and the concert hall is extensive – spanning opera, ballet and symphonic works.

Mariss Jansons

Latvian, born in 1943, Jansons is the Music Director of the Royal Concertgebouw Orchestra and the Chief Conductor of the Bavarian Radio

Symphony Orchestra. And it's in his blood too: 'As a very small boy, three years old, I was always observing . . . I went to my father's rehearsals. When I came home, I put my book on the table and started to conduct.'

Sir Antonio Pappano

Despite his Italian parentage, Antonio Pappano was actually born in Epping in Essex, although his family moved to Connecticut in the US when he was a teenager. A huge success as Music Director of the Royal Opera House, he holds the same role at the Orchestra dell'Accademia Nazionale di Santa Cecilia and has also been Principal Guest Conductor of the Israel Philharmonic Orchestra.

Vasily Petrenko

The young Russian in charge of the Royal Liverpool Philharmonic Orchestra has been making waves in the classical music world ever since he arrived on Merseyside. Petrenko's vigorous and energetic style is also perfectly suited to his Principal Conductorship of the National Youth Orchestra of Great Britain. He is also the Chief Conductor of the Oslo Philharmonic Orchestra.

Sir Simon Rattle

Quite possibly the best-known British classical musician of his generation, this Liverpudlian made his conducting debut with the Royal Liverpool Philharmonic Orchestra while he was still at school. Rattle sprang to international fame for his work with the City of Birmingham Symphony Orchestra. His status as a classical superstar was cemented when he was appointed Music Director of the Berlin Philharmonic in 2002. He also regularly conducts the Vienna Philharmonic, the Philadelphia Orchestra and the Orchestra of the Age of Enlightenment.

Esa-Pekka Salonen

Born in 1958, this Finnish conductor and composer, currently the Chief Conductor and Artistic Advisor of the Philharmonia Orchestra and Conductor Laureate of the Los Angeles Philharmonic, is noted for his passionate and exacting style. He is also a respected contemporary classical composer, often premiering his own works with his orchestras.

three

The String Section

Violin

The crowned king of string instruments, the violin section makes up a third of the modern symphony orchestra, the largest of any section. They are divided into two groups: the first violins and the second violins. As with all the parts of the orchestra, each group of violins has a principal player, who sits at the front of the group. The principal first violinist is usually known as the leader (occasionally the term 'concertmaster' is used). He or she is the senior regular player in the orchestra and works particularly closely with the conductor.

As an instrument, the violin has a fantastic range of around four octaves and, because of its compact size and the way in which it is played, it is capable of amazing agility. It was developed, in the way we know it today, in the sixteenth century and enjoyed a golden period in the seventeenth century, a situation that gives rise to the deified status of instruments of the period, notably those made by Antonio Stradivari.

Here are four masters of the violin-making world:

Stradivari

Sometimes known by the Latin version of his name (Stradivarius), Antonio Stradivari is considered the greatest of all violin-makers. Known affectionately as 'Strads' and prized for their amazing tone (particularly those made between 1698 and 1725), his violins sell for art-world prices. In 2011, the auction house Tarisio sold a Stradivarius, nicknamed 'Lady Blunt', for $15.9 million.

Guarneri

A family of violin-makers (the technical term is luthiers) who, like Stradivari, worked out of Cremona in the seventeenth and early eighteenth centuries. In 2008, Sotheby's sold a Guarneri, previously owned by the Belgian composer Henri Vieuxtemps, for 'well in excess' of the previous record held by a Stradivarius nicknamed 'The Hammer', which was sold for $3.54 million at Christie's in 2006.

Amati

The earliest of the great violin-makers, the head of the family, Andrea (born in 1505), is thought to have given the modern violin its style. His grandson Nicolò is likely to have taught Stradivari himself.

Montagnana

Sometimes known as 'the Mighty Venetian', Domenico Montagana (born in 1686) is also famed for his cellos. He worked from a small shop close to the Rialto Bridge in Venice.

Viola

If the string instruments of the orchestra were singers (soprano at the top followed by alto, tenor and bass), the viola would be the alto. Born at roughly the same time as the violin, it has a more mellow, burnished tone than its counterpart, which can tend to sound shrill in comparison. With its four strings – tuned to C, G, D and A, five notes below those of the violin – it has not been favoured as much by composers in terms of concertos, although there is still a fine body of work for the instrument. Hector Berlioz's *Harold in Italy* was commissioned by the great Niccolò Paganini as a concerto for viola – the instrument was his passion at the time. William Walton's *Viola Concerto* was given its premiere performance in 1929 by composer Paul Hindemith, who was also a concert violist and himself wrote a number of orchestral works featuring the instrument.

Cello

An abbreviation of the word 'violoncello', this member of the string family is bigger than a viola, but smaller than a double-bass. It is played between the performer's knees, which has spawned a whole host of double entendres down the years from conductors. ('Madam, you have between your legs a fine instrument which could bring pleasure to a lot of men and all you can do is scratch it,' from Sir Thomas Beecham particularly comes to mind.) The composers Luigi Boccherini and Jacques Offenbach were both masterly cellists and the twentieth century produced such greats as England's Jacqueline du Pré, Spain's Pablo Casals, France's Paul Tortelier and Russia's Mstislav Rostropovich. We are lucky to have a string of modern-day masters including Steven Isserlis and Yo-Yo Ma performing today. Until recently, this list also included Julian Lloyd Webber, who sadly had to announce his retirement as a cellist in 2014, due to a neck injury.

Double-bass

Big in size and big in sound, the double-bass is the largest string instrument in the orchestra – and it also reaches down to the lowest notes among the strings. Although not always the case, it is usually played with a bow in an orchestral setting. In the jazz world, where it is referred to as a 'string bass', it tends to be plucked and fulfils much the same role as a bass guitar does in a rock band. Usually relegated to the back of the orchestra, it does very occasionally get to be the star of the show. The Austrian composer Karl Ditters von Dittersdorf wrote no fewer than two concertos for the double-bass. It also gets an outing as the elephant in Camille Saint-Saëns' *Carnival of the Animals.*

four

The Brass Section

A quick note here to remind you that brass instruments don't have to be made of brass, just as woodwind instruments don't have to be made of wood. The common feature for the instruments that make up the brass section is a cupped mouthpiece, which looks like a small fat chalice. It is plugged into one end of the instrument. When players blow into the mouthpiece, they vibrate their lips across it to produce a sound.

Trumpet

To call the trumpet a lip-vibrated cylindrical bore aerophone, while being technically accurate, would not begin to convey the impressive range of colours that it can produce. This is an instrument that can range from attention-grabbing authority to haunting, elegiac beauty. The modern trumpet is the undisputed leader of the brass section, a full eight feet of coiled tubing, whose every note is produced via just three valves and the ever-changing lipwork (called embouchure) of the player's mouth.

Trumpets, like many brass instruments, are transposing instruments, which means that the note we hear is different from the pitch indicated in the score. The most common trumpet is in B flat, which means that the note C in the score will sound as B flat.

Many bridegrooms have had the hairs on the back of their necks raised in a mixture of apprehension and relief at the start of a rousing trumpet voluntary. Despite originally being pieces for the organ (which made a feature out of using the trumpet stop), they are very often used at weddings, arranged for trumpet or not, to signal the bride's arrival and hopefully elegant procession down the aisle.

French Horn

Uncoil the French horn and you would have eleven feet of brass piping in your hands. Originating in the world of hunting, the horn started to make an appearance in the world of orchestral music in France around the time of Jean-Baptiste Lully, in the seventeenth century. Valves were added in 1827 and composers such as Robert Schumann and Richard Wagner were big fans of this more modern instrument. The effect of the valves was to make it an easier instrument to play, as the performers no longer had to create all of the different notes with their embouchure. Modern French horns are made in five parts: the main body, the mouthpiece, the 'bell' (the round part the player sticks his or her hand up), the mouth pipe and the valves. French horns make a wonderful sound: when they are played softly, they can sound pastoral and placid, and when they are loud, they can be menacing and regal.

Trombone

Somehow, it seems strangely apt that the trombone, an occasionally sliding comic piece of equipment, should be descended from an early English instrument called the 'shagbolt' (or sackbut). It is essentially a length of brass tubing whose notes are changed by lengthening the tube with a slide, in a range of seven positions. Mozart used trombones to great effect in his opera *Don Giovanni*, but their first ever use in a symphony came when Beethoven chose to include them in his *Symphony No. 5*. They possess a stout and, let's not deny it, loud sound, useful for its ability to penetrate, but equally at home in a proud, perhaps tragic mode, such as in the *Tuba mirum* from Mozart's *Requiem*.

Tuba

This benevolent-sounding bass brass instrument comprises that cup-shaped mouthpiece again, along with around 18 feet of coiled tubing and, usually, four valves (there can be anything from three to six). Despite being principally a bass instrument – it can reach nearly an octave lower than the standard bass singing voice – it also possesses an impressive upper register stretching into the high male tenor range. This versatility has made it an extremely useful instrument for composers since its introduction in around 1835. Ralph Vaughan Williams wrote his *Tuba Concerto* in 1954 for the London Symphony Orchestra's then principal tuba, Philip Catelinet. It soon became one of the composer's surprise hits.

five

The Woodwind Section

Flute

Flutes go back to ancient Egyptian times and beyond. Variants of the instrument are also present in areas of world music, but here we are concentrating on flutes used in the Western classical music tradition.

Despite being part of the woodwind family, the flute is now rarely made of wood, instead being manufactured from metal. The instrument was originally known as the 'transverse flute' or the 'German flute'. It was given the first name because it was designed to be played sideways, unlike, say, a recorder (which was sometimes known as the 'English flute'). The second epithet came about because the instrument seems to have hailed from Germany in the distant past.

Flutes are distinct from other woodwind instruments because they have no reed. The player simply blows into the metal tube and creates the notes via the finger holes positioned along the length of the instrument. The flute's range runs over three octaves upwards from middle C, hitting the high notes with ease.

Famous flautists (the correct name for a flute player) include Sir James Galway, who was a massive hit in the 1970s and 1980s as 'the man with the golden flute' and Emmanuel Pahud, currently the principal flautist of the Berlin Philharmonic Orchestra.

Piccolo

A quick word here for the piccolo, which is a half-size flute. It operates in the same way as its bigger cousin, but it makes a sound an octave higher than written – so it's just like a flute, but it can hit stratospherically high notes, adding a lovely sparkling sound at the top of the woodwind section.

Oboe

This member of the woodwind family is the instrument to which all others in the orchestra tune. This is because it can be heard easily above the rest and also because it holds its note very well. It gets its name from the French words *haut* (high) and *bois* (wood).

It is a 'double-reed' instrument, which means that the oboist makes a sound by blowing across two reeds stuck together (rather than just one on its own), at the same time uncovering or covering the holes on the instrument's body with his or her fingers. The metal attachments (which look a little like jewellery) allow the player to open and close the holes with ease. The oboe's interior chamber is conical, rather than cylindrical like that of flutes and clarinets, and this gives it its unique sound.

The instrument has been a popular choice for concerto composers: Albinoni, Vivaldi and Mozart all wrote particularly fine examples. In more modern times, Ravel wrote a starring role for the oboe in his celebrated *Boléro*, while Richard Strauss's *Oboe Concerto* was one of his last masterpieces.

Cor anglais

Although its name translates literally as 'English horn', this member of the woodwind family of instruments is neither English nor a horn. Many people mistakenly think that it must be part of the brass section, but it resides firmly in the woodwind section of the orchestra. It is actually a tenor version of the oboe.

According to one theory, it got its rather strange name because early tenor-oboe audiences thought that it sounded like angels. The German word for 'angel' is *Engel*, but somehow the true meaning was lost in translation and it ended up being called 'English horn'. Funnily enough, we always refer to it in French, just to confuse matters further. It looks like an oboe, except that it is slightly bigger with a bulbous bell. It has a particularly alluring sound, which is shown off well in Dvořák's *Symphony No. 9* (*'From the New World'*).

Clarinet

Unlike the oboe, which has a double reed, the clarinet is a single-reed instrument. It originated around 1690, but the version we know today came into being only towards the middle of the nineteenth century. Mozart was the first composer to use the clarinet in a symphony. Clarinets come in a whole host of different varieties, so it is important to know which one is which.

The clarinet that appears in most orchestral

settings is usually pitched in the key of B flat – which means that when it plays a written C in the music, it actually sounds as a B flat, one note lower. There is also a range of other clarinets in, variously, A, E flat, D and F – as well as a bass clarinet – each of which plays their sounded notes at a different pitch from their written notes.

Then there is the pedal clarinet, also known as the contrabass clarinet or the double-bass clarinet, which tends to be played only in military bands. The clarina, heckelclarina, heckelclarinette and holztrompete are musical curiosities. They are clarinet-related instruments, but only very rarely make an appearance.

Bassoon

This rather large, elongated wooden instrument is the second-lowest of all the woodwind instruments; the lowest being its close relation, the double-bassoon, which is also known as the contra-bassoon. The bassoon is another 'double-reed' instrument. Its body is basically two conical pieces of wood (usually maple or Brazilian rosewood), with a 'hairpin' design allowing the tube through which the sound travels to double back on itself. One of the instrument's many claims to fame is that it stars as the musical voice of the grandfather in Prokofiev's *Peter and the Wolf*.

Saxophone

Born and raised in Belgium, Adolphe Sax was in his late twenties and living in Paris when he invented his saxophone in the 1840s. Like a clarinet, it is a wind instrument with a single-reed mouthpiece. However, unlike a clarinet, it has a fairly simple fingering system. It has a 'conical bore' (i.e. it is wider at the bottom than it is at the top) and is very popular in military bands, not to mention jazz groups.

The Russian composer Alexander Glazunov loved the sound the saxophone produced and wrote his *Concerto for Alto Saxophone and Strings* in 1934 after repeated requests from Sigurd Raschèr, a legendary German-born saxophonist, who later had a successful career in the US with over 200 concert works for the saxophone dedicated to him.

In more modern times, the combination of medieval plainchant and improvised jazz brought together by the saxophonist Jan Garbarek and the Hilliard Ensemble, a noted early music vocal group, for the album *Officium* in 1993 has proved to be an enduring Classic FM listeners' favourite.

six

The Percussion Section

Percussion instruments are struck by sticks of all kinds, or by a hand or a pedal. They are generally thought to be the second oldest instruments on the planet, beaten when it comes to making music only by the human voice. The percussion family can be divided into two parts: those instruments with a set pitch and those without. Examples of the former include timpani, xylophones and glockenspiels, while triangles, tambourines and castanets fall into the second category. There is a whole host of other weird and wonderful objects that composers have dreamed up for the percussion section to play, including car horns and assorted pieces of metal in different shapes and sizes.

For a long time, percussion instruments tended

to be used in Western classical music more for colour, rhythm and other specific musical effects than for anything else. However, over recent years, they have emerged as instruments in their own right. Artists such as Evelyn Glennie and Colin Currie have done an enormous amount to raise percussionists' standing and also to grow the repertoire through the commissioning of new, often spectacular works.

Various keyboard and string instruments are placed alongside the percussion section within the orchestra:

Harpsichord and Clavichord

This small keyboard was the forerunner of the piano. The main difference between the two instruments is that the harpsichord does not hammer the strings inside its casing as a piano does. Instead, it plucks them with a pin. The inner workings of a harpsichord contain a series of forty-eight strings, each with its own pin plucker, and a spruce or cedar soundboard, which helps to amplify the sound. Another related instrument is the clavichord, which hits its strings with metal blades called tangents, which stay in position until the keys are released. The volume produced depends on how hard a player can strike the keys. Although harpsichords are still played today, the invention of the piano rendered them far less popular than they were in Baroque times and they remain an instrument that listeners tend either to love or to hate.

Piano

When the piano came along, it solved a problem that faced many eighteenth-century keyboard players: the lack of the ability of the clavichord and harpsichord to play both loudly and softly. There was no sense of light and shade in performances on these instruments. The man who changed all that was an Italian called Bartolomeo Cristofori. He was born in Padua in 1655 and was possibly a cello- or violin-maker. While working in Florence for Duke Ferdinand de' Medici, he produced a keyboard with an action that used hammers to allow the strings either to resonate or not, depending on whether the player wanted them to. The hammers then returned to their prone position, ready to be hit again. This gave the new instrument both agility and volume. That unique selling point – the 'nuova inventione che fa'il piano e il forte', as Cristofori put it at the time – led to the instrument gaining the name 'pianoforte', which translates as 'quiet loud'. Today, this has been shortened simply to 'piano'.

One way of placing the invention of the piano within the history of classical music is to look at the works of Haydn (born 1732) and Mozart (born 1756). That twenty-odd year difference meant that Haydn wrote a dozen keyboard concertos while Mozart penned twenty-seven piano concertos. The latter was one of the first composers to realise the potential of the new pianoforte, writing a stunning body of work that exploited all of its possibilities. Alongside the concertos – Mozart's calling-card showpieces, which he frequently used to gain work in a new town or to show what he could do for a new patron – are the eighteen piano sonatas, which demonstrate virtually every facet of the instrument.

Mozart's favourite instruments were a Stein piano made in Augsburg and one built by Walter of Vienna, which is on display at the composer's birthplace museum in Salzburg. If you ever see it, you will notice that Mozart had to work with twenty-two fewer notes than there are on a modern piano. Pianos now have eighty-eight notes, whereas Mozart's Walter had just sixty-six. Pedals were not always pedals, either. The job done by today's 'soft' pedal was often achieved by means of a knob, positioned on the front of the case, which the player would pull by hand. Intriguingly, a few years before Mozart was born, Johann Sebastian Bach was shown the new pianoforte and treated to a demonstration of all it could do, but decided it was not for him.

You might occasionally hear mention of a 'prepared piano'. This does not refer to an instrument that has been tuned and given the once over with furniture polish and a vigorous rubbing with a duster. The term 'prepared piano' was coined by twentieth-century composer John Cage. In this instance, the piano is prepared by having items placed inside the case on the strings. These could range from spoons, to bells, to nuts and bolts. The object is to trigger not only the notes of the piano but a series of extraneous random sounds, too. Cage's *Sonatas and Interludes* are still considered the benchmark in this area.

Celesta

This unusual instrument looks and sounds a little like a baby's piano. Invented in 1886 by Auguste Mustel, it uses metal plates struck by hammers to make its heavenly sound. As soon as he saw the new instrument in Paris, Tchaikovsky was desperate to be the first Russian to use it and it featured in *The Dance of the Sugar Plum Fairy* from his ballet *The Nutcracker*. Mahler was the first composer to use the celesta in a symphony (his sixth). It is widely employed by modern-day film composers, such as John Williams, who used its magical sound in the hit tune *'Hedwig's Theme'* from his *Harry Potter* soundtrack.

Harp

This is an instrument that has been in existence since ancient times and has developed in many different shapes and sizes over the years. The modern concert harp usually has 46 or 47 strings, which gives it a range of six-and-a-half octaves. That is not quite as much as a piano, but is still pretty wide-ranging: it means that a harp can play notes as deep as a double-bass and as high as a piccolo. Harps also have pedals, which the harpists press once to raise the string up one semitone and then press again to raise it up another semitone. The need for simultaneous hand and foot co-ordination makes it an incredibly hard instrument to play, while keeping a harp in tune is almost a full-time job in itself. In 2001, the Prince of Wales re-established the position of court harpist. The first holder of the title was Catrin Finch, with the subsequent court harpists being Jemima Phillips, Claire Jones and Hannah Stone.

Organ

A word here for an instrument that, although it is not strictly part of the orchestra, should be included in this book because of its contribution to many great orchestral works, whether it be Tchaikovsky's *1812 Overture* or Saint-Saëns' *Symphony No. 3*, where it is very much the star of the show.

The organ is a monster of an instrument, often employing up to five keyboards (known as manuals), a pedal board and sometimes more than a hundred stops. Although born in ancient Greece (where water was often used to create the necessary pressure), it was in the sixth and seventh centuries that an air-bellowed version of the organ began to come into its own. By J. S. Bach's time, a golden age of organ building had led to a mass of complex music being written for what was then regarded as a high-tech instrument. If you ever have the opportunity to check out the organ in the Royal Albert Hall in

London, you should seize it. The instrument was overhauled and rebuilt in 2002. It has 147 stops and an amazing 9,997 pipes.

Guitar

Some people might not include our final instrument in a book about the orchestra at all, but at Classic FM we think that, like the organ, it has earned its place in an orchestral round-up. Although the guitar is a string instrument and a classical music instrument at that, it is not usually considered as being a string instrument in the orchestral sense – mainly because, unlike the violin, cello and double-bass, it is never played with a bow. The guitar that we know today is actually a member of the lute family. It has six strings, which are tuned to E, A, D, G, B and E. The back and sides of a good guitar are usually made of Brazilian rosewood; the neck is cedar; the fingerboard is ebony; and the face is spruce. Over the years composers such as Boccherini, Paganini and Berlioz composed for the instrument. Probably the greatest guitar work of all was written by the Spaniard Joaquín Rodrigo – the *Concierto de Aranjuez*. It became a staple part of the repertoire for two great guitar virtuosos in the latter part of the twentieth century: the Englishman Julian Bream and the Australian John Williams. Today, it is now often played by the two men who continue to ensure that guitar music remains at the forefront of classical music lovers' minds: the Australian Craig Ogden and the Montenegrin Miloš Karadaglić.

seven

Great British Orchestras

So, now you know what makes up an orchestra in instrumental terms, let's turn our attention to some of the finest orchestral institutions around the UK. In no way is this intended to be a complete list of all of the orchestras that perform week in and week out around the country. Instead, we've concentrated on the ones that you're most likely to hear being played on Classic FM, and that includes a very good cross section of the nation's great symphony and chamber orchestras.

Academy of Ancient Music

When the conductor Christopher Hogwood founded the Academy of Ancient Music back in 1973, he wanted to perform music from the

Baroque and Classical periods in exactly the way that the composers had originally intended it to be heard. That meant that the instruments themselves needed to be authentic, so out went steel strings and in came strings made of animal gut; valves on trumpets and chin rests on violins and violas were jettisoned; and the cellists had to forgo spikes to rest their instruments on the floor, squeezing them between their legs instead. The sound was very different from that of a modern orchestra and it excited audiences and critics alike. The *Independent* described the Academy of Ancient Music as 'the ultimate raspberry to anyone who says Baroque music is predictable'. In 2006, Richard Egarr took over as Music Director and the orchestra continues to flourish – it now has more than 300 recordings to its name.

Academy of St Martin in the Fields

Founded by the violinist Neville Marriner in 1958, the Academy of St Martin in the Fields performs in a church of the same name just off Trafalgar Square in London. It is among the most recorded of all British orchestras, with more than 500 discs under its belt and it had a particularly busy period in the recording studio with the advent of the compact disc in the 1980s. Initially, it was formed by the musicians on a collegiate basis, without a conductor. But a couple of years after its launch, Marriner (now Sir Neville) laid down his violin and took up the conductor's baton. The orchestra varies in size from chamber to symphonic strength.

Aurora Orchestra

Despite only being a decade old, the Aurora Orchestra has cut an impressive swathe through the classical music world, quickly establishing itself as a chamber orchestra to be reckoned with. Its Artistic Director Nicholas Collon is also making something of a name for himself, with a burgeoning career conducting many other major orchestras. It's no mean feat to establish a brand-new orchestra in London – and to get the classical music establishment and audiences to take notice of what you are doing in the concert hall. Aurora has managed to do this in style, making its home at the recently built Kings Place Concert Hall just around the corner from King's Cross station and also at LSO St Luke's, an innovative education, rehearsal, recording and small concert venue in a converted Grade-I-listed Hawksmoor church, near the Barbican Centre in the City of London. As well as being comfortable performing seasons of Bach and Mozart, the orchestra has built a reputation for developing cutting-edge creative partnerships with other art forms, including dance, film and theatre. Definitely one to listen out for in the future.

Britten Sinfonia

Launched in 1992, the Britten Sinfonia might not be the oldest orchestra in this book – but it has certainly made an indelible mark for the better on the country's chamber music life. Unusually, it does not have a permanent principal conductor or music director. Instead, this role is taken by a series of different guest artists with whom the orchestra collaborates, often performing without anyone taking the traditional conducting role at all. The Britten Sinfonia's work is centred in the East of England, where it has residencies in Cambridge and Norwich, but its performances are by no means limited to these regions, with regular concerts in Brighton, at the Barbican Centre in London and also across the European mainland. The orchestra has diversified to include the choral group Britten Sinfonia

Voices and the Britten Sinfonia Academy, which trains school-age musicians at weekends.

Bournemouth Symphony Orchestra

Bournemouth's celebrated orchestra is not actually based in Bournemouth. Its home in fact is just down the road in Poole. It started life in the 1890s, when Sir Dan Godfrey was appointed to form a new municipal orchestra, drawing players from the Italian military band that for many years had given concerts in the town. Because of this, the orchestra still played in military uniform for the first few years of its life. It was called the Bournemouth Municipal Orchestra until 1954, when it was given its current name.

The BSO has a long pedigree of championing English music; when it celebrated its 25th anniversary, the likes of Sir Edward Elgar sent letters of congratulation to mark its achievements in this area. Today, the BSO is Classic FM's Orchestra in the South of England, performing more than 130 concerts a year in venues including Basingstoke, Bournemouth, Bristol, Exeter, Poole, Portsmouth, Southampton, Weymouth and Winchester. It was notable in being the first British orchestra to appoint a female principal conductor – Marin

Alsop, who directed the orchestra from 2002 to 2008. The dynamic young Ukrainian Kirill Karabits took up the baton at the beginning of the 2009 season.

City of Birmingham Symphony Orchestra

The Birmingham Symphony Orchestra was founded in 1920 and renamed the City of Birmingham Symphony Orchestra twenty-eight years later. There is a long tradition of classical music in the city, with a regular music festival dating back as far as 1768. The current Music Director is Andris Nelsons but it was the then twenty-five-year-old Simon Rattle who made his name with the orchestra when he took charge in 1980. Under his leadership, the CBSO developed a strong reputation both at home and abroad and recorded extensively. In 1991, the city benefited from the opening of a brand-new purpose-built concert venue in the heart of Birmingham. Symphony Hall remains one of the finest places anywhere to listen to classical music, with world-class acoustics. It is run by the same team that operates Birmingham's Town Hall as a smaller classical music venue just down the road.

City of London Sinfonia

The City of London Sinfonia was founded by the conductor Richard Hickox in 1971. He remained its Music Director until his death in 2008. The orchestra is particularly committed to the performance of the music of twentieth century and contemporary British composers; it has made more than 130 recordings of their music.

Although the City of London Sinfonia has toured as far afield as Australia, Brazil, China, Colombia, Dubai and Norway, it has specialised in taking world-class live classical music to English locations that might not otherwise experience it at all, including Chatham, High Wycombe, Ipswich and King's Lynn. It is not to be confused with either the Sinfonia of London, a studio orchestra founded by the Rank Organisation in 1955, or the London Sinfonietta, a completely separate contemporary music orchestra.

Hallé Orchestra

Founded in Manchester in 1858 by the respected pianist and conductor Charles Hallé, the Hallé Orchestra is the UK's second oldest continuously operating professional symphony orchestra, beaten to the title of being the oldest only by its near neighbour the Royal Liverpool Philharmonic, which can trace its origin as a professional band back to 1853. The Hallé's home venue is the wonderful Bridgewater Hall in the centre of Manchester and the orchestra has a long association with the cities of Bradford and Sheffield. The orchestra is currently enjoying a sustained artistic resurgence under Music Director Sir Mark Elder. He follows in a long line of prestigious principal conductors, including Sir Thomas Beecham, Sir Hamilton Harty, Hans Richter and Sir John Barbirolli. The orchestra's list of world-premiere performances includes Elgar's *Symphony No. 1*, Vaughan Williams' *Sinfonia Antartica* and Finzi's *Cello Concerto*.

London Mozart Players

The London Mozart Players have become famous for doing one thing and doing it very well – namely, playing the music of Haydn, Mozart, Beethoven, Schubert and their contemporaries. The orchestra was founded in 1949 by the violinist Harry Blech, who set out to take the finest conductors, soloists and players to regional concert halls and small-scale venues in out-of-the-way places right around the country. The music directors who followed on from Blech – Jane Glover, Matthias Bamert, Andrew Parrott and Gérard Korsten – have each continued in this tradition. They have also maintained the purity of the London Mozart Players' central philosophy of performing music only from the Classical period. In a crowded market of London orchestras this has given the London Mozart Players a very clear point of difference.

London Philharmonic Orchestra

Sir Thomas Beecham founded the London Philharmonic Orchestra in 1932, with his new ensemble giving its first concert at the Queen's Hall in London that same year. Just seven years later, with the outbreak of the Second World War, it ran into financial difficulties and was saved from bankruptcy only by its players, who took over its running. The LPO's notable international achievements include being the first British orchestra to appear in Soviet Russia (in 1956) and being the first Western orchestra to visit China (in 1973). The orchestra is resident at the Royal Festival Hall in London and also spends the summer as the resident orchestra at Glyndebourne Festival

Opera deep in the Sussex countryside – a role it has undertaken since 1964.

The LPO is also particularly successful in the cinema, with its soundtrack recordings including *The Lord of the Rings* trilogy, *Lawrence of Arabia* and *The Mission*. After Beecham, its principal conductors have included Sir Adrian Boult, Sir Bernard Haitink, Sir Georg Solti, Klaus Tennstedt, Kurt Masur and the present incumbent Vladimir Jurowski – one of a new generation of young conductors who are galvanising the British orchestral scene.

London Sinfonietta

Co-founded by impresario Nicholas Snowman and conductor David Atherton in 1968, this chamber orchestra has focused on modern classical music throughout its life, with many of its performances including world premieres of key works by living composers The orchestra has never been afraid to push the boundaries of how a classical music concert should look and sound, on occasions blending in electronic music and working with folk and jazz musicians. Other major collaborations have included pieces involving choreographed dance and specially shot film. In 1969, the orchestra gave the premiere performance of John Tavener's *The Whale*, recording the work for the Beatles' Apple Records label the following year. Tavener ended up on the label after his brother had worked as a builder on Ringo Starr's house. Today, the London Sinfonietta is resident at London's Southbank Centre and is based at Kings Place. It has enjoyed a particularly close relationship with the composer and conductor Oliver Knussen.

London Symphony Orchestra

Widely acknowledged as being among the greatest orchestras in the world, the LSO is a self-governing ensemble, which came into being in 1904 after a group of players fell out with the conductor Sir Henry Wood and resigned en masse from his Queen's Hall Orchestra. The new orchestra was owned and governed by the players, along the lines of the Berlin Philharmonic Orchestra, which had come into existence around twenty years earlier.

The LSO's first conductor was the legendary Hans Richter. In the years since, the orchestra has been conducted by a *Who's Who* of top baton-wavers including Richard Strauss, Sir Thomas

Beecham, Leopold Stokowski, Sir John Barbirolli, Benjamin Britten, Leonard Bernstein, André Previn, Claudio Abbado, Sir Colin Davis, Michael Tilson Thomas and Valery Gergiev.

The orchestra has mounted extensive international tours ever since it became the first British orchestra to tour abroad, to Paris, in 1906. Six years later, the LSO was the first British orchestra to visit the USA, narrowly avoiding travelling on the *Titanic*. In 1956, it was the first British orchestra to visit South Africa and, in 1963, it was the first to visit Japan. The LSO's first world tour was in 1964, taking in Israel, Turkey, Iran, India, Hong Kong, Korea, Japan and the US.

For many people, the LSO has become synonymous with film soundtracks – it has provided the musical accompaniment to all of the *Star Wars* movies. In the late 1970s, the orchestra gained a significant financial boost from its series of *Classic Rock* recordings, which proved to be an enormous commercial success. In the strictly classical world, the LSO's recording of Elgar's *Cello Concerto*, with Jacqueline du Pré as soloist and Sir John Barbirolli as conductor, is regarded by many as being the greatest version of the work ever committed to disc.

Today, the LSO is Classic FM's orchestra in the City of London, resident at the Barbican Centre and at St Luke's.

Manchester Camerata

Another leading chamber orchestra, Manchester Camerata, reaches audiences of 70,000 people every year with residencies at the Bridgewater Hall and the Royal Northern College of Music in its home city, as well as regular appearances in towns and cities as varied as Blackburn, Bolton, Bridlington, Chester, Colne, Hanley, Hull, Kendal, Lancaster, Leeds, Malvern, Sheffield, Stafford and Ulverston. Its Artistic Director is the Hungarian Gábor Takács-Nagy.

National Children's Orchestra of Great Britain

A jewel in the UK's music education crown, the National Children's Orchestra brings together the most promising young musicians aged between seven and thirteen from right across the country to perform together as a symphony orchestra. It was founded in 1978 by Vivienne Price MBE because she wanted to create an ensemble that enabled children who were younger than the normal youth-orchestra age group to perform together. It proved so successful that the National Children's Orchestra set up a training orchestra to operate alongside the main ensemble to help provide an even earlier taste of orchestral life for young musicians. The organisation's track record for spotting talent is pretty impressive, with the cellist Guy Johnston, the violinist Nicola Benedetti and the conductors Robin Ticciati and Daniel Harding all former members of the National Children's Orchestra – not to mention a legion of musicians now playing professionally in many of Britain's leading orchestras. Many of the youngsters who play in the National Children's Orchestra graduate on to the National Youth Orchestra once they become old enough.

National Youth Orchestra of Great Britain

Founded in 1948, the National Youth Orchestra set out to prove that British teenagers could form a top-quality symphony orchestra that performed core classical repertoire with proficiency and flair that belied the age of the performers. Today, the

National Youth Orchestra is the foremost training ground for the musicians who go on to make their careers in professional British orchestras. The statistics speak for themselves: one-fifth of the London Symphony Orchestra's ninety players are NYO graduates; there are thirteen former NYO players in the Philharmonia Orchestra; and the Orchestra of the Royal Opera House and the City of Birmingham Symphony Orchestra have among their ranks twelve and nine NYO alumni respectively.

The orchestra draws its players, who are all teenagers, from all corners of the British Isles, for three intensive residential sessions each year. At the end of each period, during which the players receive coaching from top professional musicians, the orchestra performs in concert, often under the baton of Principal Conductor Vasily Petrenko. In 2013, the National Youth Orchestra was awarded the Queen's Medal for Music for its significant contribution to the country's musical life. It remains one of the most important organisations for ensuring that the future of classical music in the UK continues to shine brightly. The *Guardian* has described the orchestra as 'a credit to Britain'.

Orchestra of the Age of Enlightenment

One of the more prosaically named ensembles in this book, the OAE is different from nearly all the other orchestras we feature because it tends not to play by the same set of rules as everyone else. Now, don't misunderstand us, because artistically the OAE is absolutely top notch, but it likes to be a little different. So, there's no single principal conductor running things, while the players perform on period instruments without any of the snazzy modern technological advances that would make, say, a twenty-first-century clarinet unfamiliar to a composer such as Mozart. Conductors Sir Mark Elder, Ivan Fischer, Sir Simon Rattle and Vladimir Jurowski are regular fixtures on the podium each season and the orchestra has carved out a new niche for itself with its 'Night Shift' performances that place classical music in non-traditional late-night settings, with the aim of taking the genre to a group of listeners who would otherwise quite probably never encounter classical music in a live setting at all. By the way, the 'Age of Enlightenment' was a cultural movement of European intellectuals from around the turn of the eighteenth century; they placed great emphasis on 'reason' and 'individualism', rather than on 'tradition'. They set great store by using science to question ideas that had previously been seen as unchallengeable – so it's easy to see from where the musicians behind the OAE have drawn their inspiration.

Philharmonia Orchestra

The Philharmonia Orchestra's fine reputation is all the more impressive given its relative youth. It was the brainchild of impresario and record company executive Walter Legge, who came up with the plan to establish a new virtuoso orchestra towards the end of the Second World War. It made its debut on 27 October 1945, in London's Kingsway Hall, with Sir Thomas Beecham conducting.

The connection between Beecham and the orchestra did not last for long – he disagreed with Legge over how it should be run and decided to form his own Royal Philharmonic – but other leading figures flocked to conduct it. Within a few years, the orchestra, which Legge had formed primarily to record for the record label EMI, was being conducted by no less a personage than Richard Strauss. It went on to give the world premiere of his *Four Last Songs* for soprano and orchestra in

1950. During that decade, the orchestra blossomed further, taking part in the historic opening concert of London's Royal Festival Hall in 1951 and touring Europe and the US in 1952 and 1954 respectively with Herbert von Karajan.

In 1964, Legge decided to disband the orchestra. It refused to die, instead re-emerging as the self-governing New Philharmonia Orchestra. The legendary conductor Otto Klemperer, whom Legge had appointed Principal Conductor of the Philharmonia in 1959, decided to stick by the players, as did other great conductors, notably Carlo Maria Giulini. Klemperer remained closely associated with the orchestra until his retirement in 1971. The new name stuck until 1977, when it was changed back to the Philharmonia Orchestra.

During the 1970s and 1980s, an amazing variety of conducting talents stepped onto the Philharmonia's podium: Bernard Haitink, Lorin Maazel, Vladimir Ashkenazy, Riccardo Muti and Simon Rattle were among their number. Plácido Domingo even chose to launch his conducting career with the orchestra when he took it to Spain in 1988. The current Principal Conductor and Artistic Adviser is the Finnish conductor and composer

Esa-Pekka Salonen. Today, the orchestra is known both for the extent of its touring with world-class soloists around much of the UK (hence its title 'Classic FM's Orchestra on Tour'), as well as for its highly innovative work in the digital area, with the aim of building new audiences for classical music as a whole.

Royal Northern Sinfonia

Founded by Michael Hall in 1958, this chamber orchestra was originally known as the 'Sinfonia Orchestra'. A year later, 'Northern' was added to the front of the name. Later still, 'Orchestra' was dropped from the back end of the band's title. And then, in 2013, 'Royal' was appended to the front.

The orchestra was resident at Newcastle City Hall until 2004, when it moved to its stunning new home, the Sage Gateshead, on the other side of the River Tyne. Designed by Norman Foster, this futuristic building contains two acoustically excellent concert halls, another hall used for rehearsals and a twenty-five-room music education centre. It has enjoyed artistically strong relationships with a series of impressive conducting talents, including Tamás Vásáry, Ivan Fischer, John Wilson and the current Music Director Thomas Zehetmair. As well as concerts in Gateshead, the Royal Northern Sinfonia also regularly performs in London, with international dates as far afield as Hong Kong, the Netherlands, Austria, Germany and Hungary.

Royal Liverpool Philharmonic Orchestra

It might seem surprising to some that Liverpool is the home of the country's longest-surviving professional symphony orchestra. The 'Phil' (as it is universally known on Merseyside) can trace its origins back to 1840. It became a fully professional band in 1853, five years before the UK's next-oldest symphony orchestra – the Hallé down the road in Manchester.

The orchestra was founded by a group of well-to-do merchants, who wanted to ensure that Liverpool's cultural life rivalled that of the capital. They built their own Philharmonic Hall on Hope Street in 1849. It was destroyed by fire in 1933 with a brand-new replacement opening in 1939. It is still the home of Classic FM's Orchestra in North West England today. Over the years, the list of its principal conductors has included Sir Malcolm Sargent, Sir Charles Groves, Sir John Pritchard and, in more recent times, the eminent Czech conductor Libor Pešek.

The Royal Liverpool Philharmonic has been a prolific recording orchestra. In the days of 78s, there were famous versions of Handel's *Messiah* and Elgar's *The Dream of Gerontius,* both conducted by Sargent. Later, it made pioneering first recordings of English works – notably by Delius and Bax – under the batons of Groves and Vernon Handley. It made a notable cycle of the Beethoven symphonies, conducted by Sir Charles Mackerras. More recently, the orchestra's current Chief Conductor, the dynamic young Russian Vasily Petrenko, has produced a critically acclaimed series of recordings of the Shostakovich symphonies. The orchestra is also particularly well respected for its music education work, not least for its 'In Harmony' project in a school in West Everton. This is based on Venezuela's 'El Sistema', which sees children completely immersed in the life of a symphony orchestra throughout their schooling.

Royal Philharmonic Orchestra

Founded in 1946 by the flamboyant conductor Sir Thomas Beecham, the Royal Philharmonic

Orchestra is based in London at Chelsea's Cadogan Hall, though it also gives regular performances at the Royal Albert Hall and at the Royal Festival Hall. The orchestra's debut performance was at the Davis Theatre in Croydon and it has continued to perform in the town ever since. The RPO also visits Crawley, Hull, Lowestoft, Northampton and Reading on a regular basis.

Beecham made the orchestra one of the world's great bands. After his death in 1961, which the orchestra managed to survive, it turned to other notable conductors, including Antal Doráti, Rudolf Kempe, André Previn, Walter Weller and Daniele Gatti. The current Artistic Director is Charles Dutoit. The RPO has enjoyed a long partnership with the concert promoter Raymond Gubbay, often featuring in his 'Classical Spectacular' concerts. It has recorded extensively and streams its entire Cadogan Hall concert series over the Internet.

Royal Scottish National Orchestra

Originally known simply as 'The Scottish Orchestra', the Royal Scottish National Orchestra was founded in 1891. Over the years, it has been conducted by an impressive list of great musicians, not least

Sir John Barbirolli and George Szell, but, aptly enough, it was thanks to the leadership of the Scottish-born Sir Alexander Gibson that the orchestra really flowered to win international renown.

From 1959, Gibson conducted the orchestra for twenty-five years, becoming the longest-serving music director in the orchestra's history. Under him, the orchestra became famous for its performances of Scandinavian music, notably that of Sibelius and Carl Nielsen. Gibson also took the orchestra into the pit when he founded Scottish Opera. In 1991, the orchestra was granted permission to add 'Royal' to its title (it had been renamed the Scottish National Orchestra in 1950).

Today, under its Music Director Peter Oundjian, the home of Classic FM's Orchestra in Scotland is still Glasgow, in a brand-new building right next door to the city's Royal Concert Hall. However, it also performs regularly in Aberdeen, Dundee, Edinburgh, Inverness and Perth. Its recording reputation is particularly impressive with eight Grammy nominations between 2002 and 2009. The orchestra is increasingly outward-facing in international terms, as it represents Scotland on its regular tours overseas.

Scottish Chamber Orchestra

A relative newcomer in musical circles, the Scottish Chamber Orchestra was founded in 1974. It performs throughout Scotland, touring the Highlands and Islands as well as the southern part of the country each year. Further commitments to the Edinburgh, East Neuk and St Magnus Festivals have ensured that it is heard by a wide fan base. Conductors have included Jukka-Pekka Saraste and its Conductor Laureate, Sir Charles Mackerras. The orchestra's present Principal Conductor is London-born Robin Ticciati.

Sinfonia Cymru

Founded in 1996, Sinfonia Cymru set out to do two things: to support young musicians at the start of their careers and to ensure that great classical music is heard in concert halls right across Wales. Its Music Director is Gareth Jones and the orchestra regularly performs with artists as wide-ranging as conductor Carlo Rizzi, harpist Catrin Finch and violinist Bartosz Woroch.

Southbank Sinfonia

Southbank Sinfonia bridges the gap for professional

musicians between the time when they finish their training at a music conservatoire and being offered their first job as part of a professional orchestra. Every year, a group of mostly twenty-something musicians from around the world come together in the Waterloo area of London, on the south bank of the River Thames, for a nine-month programme of performance and professional development, led by Music Director Simon Over, as well as other distinguished conductors. The Southbank Sinfonia can often be heard on Classic FM accompanying performances by the Parliament Choir, which is made up of members of both the House of Commons and House of Lords.

Ulster Orchestra

Northern Ireland's pre-eminent symphony orchestra gives as many as ninety performances each year in Belfast, Derry/Londonderry and in London and Dublin. The orchestra's main concert season takes place in the Ulster Hall and the Belfast Waterfront Hall. The Ulster Orchestra is unique among the main home-grown symphony orchestras in having a woman as its Principal Conductor. Following the trail blazed by Marin Alsop at the Bournemouth Symphony

Orchestra, JoAnn Falletta is another female American conductor who is making a name for herself this side of the Atlantic. Alas, the wait for a British-born female principal conductor at the helm of one of our great symphony orchestras is still ongoing.

eight

Great Orchestras
of the World

Just as it was with our choice of great British orchestras, the list that follows here is by no means exhaustive. It will undoubtedly be open to debate about which orchestras should or should not be included in a book like this. Space does not permit us to include every major orchestra from right around the globe. However, here are ten of Classic FM's favourite orchestras from outside the UK – and if you listen to their music or attend one of their concerts, we don't think that you will go far wrong.

Berlin Philharmonic

Founded in 1882, the same year as Tottenham Hotspur Football Club, the Berliner Philharmoniker (to give it its correct German name) is one of the world's greatest orchestras. Its list of principal conductors includes many of the greatest baton-wielders of all time, including Hans von Bülow, Richard Strauss, Wilhelm Furtwängler and Herbert von Karajan. The last is credited with improving the orchestra's already formidable reputation by transforming its sound and raising playing standards. Claudio Abbado succeeded von Karajan in 1989 and, 13 years later, the Liverpudlian conductor Sir Simon Rattle was appointed to the top job, having previously made his name at the City of Birmingham Symphony Orchestra. Critics and audiences the world over still to regard both orchestra and conductor as being at the top of their game. Today, the orchestra is continuing to build its international reputation with regular online concert broadcasts via its own interactive digital concert hall.

Chicago Symphony Orchestra

Established in 1891, the US's third-oldest symphony orchestra is now widely regarded as being America's greatest ensemble. Founded by Theodore Thomas, the orchestra even took his name for an eight-year period after his death. The orchestra's international reputation grew to new heights between 1969 and 1991 under Music Director Sir Georg Solti. On one occasion in the 1970s, the players received so much acclaim on a triumphant tour of Europe that they were given a tickertape welcome through their home city on their return. Solti handed the baton on to Daniel Barenboim in 1991, with the mighty Riccardo Muti becoming only the tenth music director in 2006. It remains an orchestra of enviable standing on the worldwide classical music stage.

Leipzig Gewandhaus Orchestra

The German city of Leipzig is one of the most influential places in classical music history. The Gewandhaus was originally a drapers' hall, which became a concert hall way back in 1781. A new hall was built in 1884, but it was damaged by Allied bombing in 1944 and was knocked down in 1968, finally being replaced in 1981. The orchestra's conductors over the years included Felix Mendelssohn from 1835 to 1847, while other greats have included: Wilhelm Furtwängler from 1922 to 1929, Kurt Masur from 1970 to 1996, and Riccardo Chailly since 2005 – he took over the music directorship of the Leipzig Opera at the same time.

Los Angeles Philharmonic

One of the greatest American orchestras, the Los Angeles Philharmonic is based at the Walt Disney Concert Hall in the winter and at the Hollywood Bowl in the summer. It was unsurprising when the Los Angeles Philharmonic came calling for Gustavo Dudamel, known to many as 'The Dude', and appointed him its Music Director. There can be few individuals who are a credible classical music performer and have a big enough personality to stand out in Tinseltown. It's testament to Dudamel's magnetic charm that he has appeared in a television advertisement for California alongside former Governor Arnold Schwarzenegger. Aside from its work in the concert hall, the LA Phil is also making a name for itself in the area of music education, with a community music programme for young people in neighbourhoods right across the city built around the Youth Orchestra Los Angeles (YOLA) project. The LA Phil records on the Deutsche Grammophon label, as well as making its concerts available across the world online, including the first full-length classical music video to be released on iTunes.

New York Philharmonic

The US's oldest symphony orchestra was founded in 1842 – almost forty years before the next-oldest American ensemble. For a period from 1928, it was known as the Philharmonic-Symphony Orchestra of New York, following a merger with the New York Symphony Orchestra. The role of the New York Philharmonic's music director is among the most coveted in classical music, with previous holders of the post including Gustav Mahler, Arturo Toscanini, Leopold Stokowski, Sir John Barbirolli, Leonard Bernstein, Pierre Boulez, Kurt Masur, Lorin Maazel and Zubin Mehta. The current Music Director is Alan Gilbert.

Royal Concertgebouw Orchestra

Concertgebouw is Dutch for 'concert building' and the Royal Concertgebouw Orchestra has the Concertgebouw in Amsterdam as its home. The orchestra came to international prominence under its second conductor, Willem Mengelberg, who was in charge for an impressive fifty years from 1895 to 1945. He was forbidden to conduct after the Second World War because of his collaboration with the Nazi occupiers of his country. More recent conductors have included Bernard Haitink and Riccardo Chailly. Mariss Jansons, regarded by some as the greatest living conductor, took over the baton in 2004. In 1988, the orchestra was granted 'Royal' status by Queen Beatrix of the Netherlands and, in 2008, *Gramophone* magazine named the Royal Concertgebouw as the top orchestra in the world.

Saint Louis Symphony Orchestra

The Saint Louis Symphony is the second-oldest American symphony orchestra, behind the New York Philharmonic. It was founded in 1880 by Dutch-born choir conductor Joseph Otten with just 31 musicians. Based in the (allegedly haunted) Powell Symphony Hall, today it is led by American-born Music Director David Robertson, who has taken the orchestra to critical heights. Other noted conductors to have stood on the podium include Itzhak Perlman and Leonard Slatkin. It was Slatkin's long musical directorship, from 1979 to 1996, that saw a real growth in the Saint Louis Symphony's musical prestige. There were problems, though. In 2001, the orchestra nearly went bankrupt, and in 2005, the musicians staged a two-month strike.

St Petersburg Philharmonic Orchestra

Russia's oldest symphony orchestra was founded in 1882, originally as the private court orchestra of Tsar Alexander III. Following the Russian Revolution in 1917, it became the State Philharmonic Orchestra of Petrograd before being named the Leningrad Philharmonic Orchestra three years later. It reverted to its original name in 1991.

The St Petersburg Philharmonic is generally regarded as one of the world's greatest orchestras, thanks in the main to conductor Evgeny Mravinsky, who was its Music Director for an amazing fifty years from 1938 to 1988. Illustrious guest conductors included Felix Weingartner, Bruno Walter and Otto Klemperer. Prokofiev premiered his piano concertos with the orchestra; it also gave the first performances of eight of Shostakovich's fifteen symphonies. The current Chief Conductor is Yuri Temirkanov.

Simón Bolívar Symphony Orchestra

The genesis for this orchestra came back in 1975, when a Venezuelan economist called José Antonio Abreu founded a music education programme in his native land, with the aim of creating a national network of orchestras for young people across the country. It became known as 'El Sistema' and four decades later it has grown to a web of 125 separate, but affiliated, orchestras. More than 300,000 children take part in the programme with the vast majority coming from economically deprived backgrounds. The Simón Bolivar Symphony Orchestra is the most famous of these Venezuelan orchestras. It first came to prominence in the UK and the USA in 2007, with its engaging young conductor Gustavo Dudamel playing a significant part in the orchestra's success. Originally made up solely of young players, these musicians are in some cases now well into their thirties, so the orchestra no longer presents itself with the word 'Youth' in its title. Despite the advancing of the years, their sound remains big and bold and their performances crackle with vibrant energy – unsurprising really, when you consider that the orchestra is twice the size of a standard symphony outfit.

Vienna Philharmonic Orchestra

Formed in 1842 by the composer Otto Nicolai, the Vienna Philharmonic is one of Europe's supreme orchestras. Its founding principles of autonomy and democracy still hold true today. It selects its own conductors and its players are all chosen from the Vienna State Opera Orchestra. The Vienna Philharmonic is resident at Vienna's amazing, gilded Musikverein concert hall and its seasons are often oversubscribed. Bookings for the famous New Year's Day concert have to be made sometimes a couple of years in advance. The orchestra has been directed by an illustrious line of great conductors, including Gustav Mahler, Wilhelm Furtwängler and Herbert von Karajan.

nine

The Music Orchestras Play

Although orchestras are involved in performing the full range of different types of classical music, from opera and ballet through to film and video-game soundtracks, with a good smattering of standalone classical works along the way, it is concertos and symphonies that tend to take up the largest part of most orchestras' waking hours.

The word 'symphony' derives from Greek, meaning 'a sounding together'. There have been various definitions of what exactly a symphony is over the years, but today we understand it to mean an extended work for orchestra. Very often, but not always, this consists of four movements; many consider it the purest musical form a composer can write.

Originally a term for any music played in a concert, the Italian word 'concerto' has now been absorbed into the English language. In modern usage, it is a musical work where music for a solo instrument is mixed and contrasted with the sound created by the rest of the orchestra.

Historians trace the introduction of the concerto back to the turn of the seventeenth century with the advent of 'concerti ecclesiastici' ('church concertos'), which pitted a group of players against the rest of the orchestra. The Italian composer Arcangelo Corelli was a major force in developing this type of composition. But it was Johann Sebastian Bach who was among the first composers to create the concerto as we know it today; in his case, making the harpsichord the solo star of the show.

Mozart took the idea and ran with it, writing concertos for dozens of different instrumental groupings. As with many of the rules surrounding classical music, very few of them are hard and fast. Although concertos occur most often for solo instruments, some composers have written for larger groupings (for example Mozart's *Flute and Harp Concerto*). It is usual for concertos to be written in three movements, but this is not always the case (Brahms's *Piano Concerto No. 2* has four movements).

Our Orchestral Top 30 to Download

Here's a list of 30 classical tracks that show off the orchestra in all of its glory. You can find them as a downloadable playlist on our website at ClassicFM.com/handyguides

Rachmaninov: *Piano Concerto No. 2 in C minor*

Written in 1900, this work marked a return to form for the composer after a savaging at the hands of the critics for his *Symphony No. 1* three years earlier. Packed full of melodies, it has regularly topped the annual Classic FM Hall of Fame poll of listeners' favourites.

Mozart: *Clarinet Concerto in A*

Written in the final year of the composer's life, for his great friend, the clarinettist Anton Stadler, whose playing was described as being 'so delicate in tone that no one who has a heart can resist it'. Cinemagoers remember it fondly for its use in the film *Out of Africa*.

Bruch: *Violin Concerto No. 1 in G minor*

This is the most famous of Bruch's three violin concertos; the composer himself recognised that this work would eclipse the rest of his output. Not always the most cheery of souls, Bruch had a tempestuous relationship with the players of the Royal Liverpool Philharmonic Orchestra, of which he was principal conductor for a brief period.

Vaughan Williams: *The Lark Ascending*

Premiered in 1921, Ralph Vaughan Williams' inspiration for this piece was a poem by George Meredith. It's a demanding work for the violin soloist to perform, with a melody that soars up into the very highest part of the instrument's register, as the lark floats away across the English countryside.

Elgar: *Cello Concerto in E minor*

Elgar was recovering from a general anaesthetic after having his tonsils out when the main tune for this piece popped into his head. It was written when he was sixty-one years old and already regarded as one of the great English composers. Many believe that the piece evokes the rolling hills of his native Worcestershire.

Beethoven: *Piano Concerto No. 5 in E flat ('Emperor')*

It wasn't Beethoven who gave this work its nick-
name, but rather one of Napoleon's officers, who
was stationed in Vienna. It is said that the soldier
declared it to be 'an emperor of a concerto'. It was
written at a time when Beethoven's musical style
was moving away from the sound of the Classical period, leaning towards the beginnings of the
Romantic era.

Beethoven: *Symphony No. 6 in F ('Pastoral')*

As its original name implies – 'Recollections of Life
in the Country' – this is a musical tribute to life out-
doors. Each of the five movements paints a picture
in sound of a particular aspect of the countryside.
This style of composition, telling a specific story,
became known as 'programme music' – and this is
one of the earliest major examples of the genre.

Elgar: *Enigma Variations*

The enigma behind these variations is one of the
great mysteries of classical music. Based on a par-
lour game between Elgar and his wife, Alice, each of
the fourteen variations refers to one of their friends.
But, even after these had been decoded, a further

enigma remained: what was the 'original theme' on which the variations are based? Elgar took the secret of it to his grave – although that hasn't prevented virtually every musicologist ever since from offering his or her own personal view on what it might be.

Beethoven: *Symphony No. 9 in D minor ('Choral')*
No list of great orchestral works would be complete without this mighty symphonic masterpiece, which is arguably the peak of Beethoven's musical accomplishment. It features a stirring choral setting of Friedrich Schiller's poem 'Ode to Joy'. It is all the more remarkable for the fact that the composer was profoundly deaf by the time the piece was premiered in 1824.

Pachelbel: *Canon in D*
Very much a 'one-hit wonder' for its Baroque composer, this work really came to prominence only in the twentieth century. It remains an extremely popular choice at weddings.

Barber: *Adagio for Strings*
This was composed originally for string quartet. Barber took the melody and turned it into a full

orchestral work a couple of years after the chamber work's debut, on the advice of the conductor Arturo Toscanini. Realising he was on to a good thing, Barber adapted it again some twenty years later, this time as a choral arrangement of the *'Agnus Dei'*.

Grieg: *Piano Concerto in A minor*

Grieg was only twenty-five years old when he composed this, one of the greatest works for piano and orchestra. It's hard to believe that this was actually the first piece he had written for a full orchestra, so confident and assured does the composition sound. Fans of the comedy duo Morecambe and Wise might well remember the piece being a central part of a sketch featuring conductor André Previn.

Saint-Saëns: *Symphony No. 3 (Organ Symphony)*

Legendary pianist virtuoso and composer Franz Liszt regarded Camille Saint-Saëns as 'the greatest organist in the world'. Two of the four movements of this work feature the organ and the composer himself believed it to be the pinnacle of his writing. It was commissioned by the Royal Philharmonic Society.

Vaughan Williams: *Fantasia on a Theme by Thomas Tallis*

Vaughan Williams wrote this piece after a period studying orchestration with the French composer Maurice Ravel in Paris. Unusually, it is scored for a large string orchestra, a slightly smaller string ensemble, and a string quartet, all playing alongside each other. The main theme is by the English Elizabethan composer Thomas Tallis.

Holst: *The Planets*

Not actually about astronomy, this work is based firmly in the world of astrology, featuring Mars, the bringer of war; Venus, the bringer of peace; Mercury, the winged messenger; Jupiter, the bringer of jollity; Saturn, the bringer of old age; Uranus, the magician; and Neptune, the mystic. It was premiered towards the end of the First World War at the Queen's Hall in London.

Dvořák: *Symphony No. 9 in E minor ('From the New World')*

The lure of a big pay cheque persuaded Dvořák to move from his native Bohemia to the USA, where he composed this symphony with its appropriate subtitle. It was premiered at New York's Carnegie Hall in 1893.

Rachmaninov: *Symphony No. 2 in E minor*

Written while he was living in Dresden, Rachmaninov's second symphony successfully avoided the critical mauling accorded to his first adventure in the genre. In fact, audiences loved it – not least because it contains what must surely be one of the most lusciously beautiful symphonic slow movements ever written.

Vivaldi: *The Four Seasons*

This is one of those pieces of core classical music that crossed over into the wider public consciousness because of a particular recording. More than two million copies of Nigel Kennedy's performance of this Baroque favourite have been sold. If you are a *Four Seasons* fan, there is a whole world of Vivaldi to discover – he composed a mind-blowing 350 concertos in total, of which 230 are for the violin.

Rodrigo: *Concierto de Aranjuez*

Although there are almost too many popular concertos for instruments such as the piano and violin to choose from when compiling a list such as this, it is rare to find a guitar concerto that is performed as part of the orchestra's regular repertoire. There is no finer example of the species than Rodrigo's seminal work, which cannot fail to conjure up images of warm Spanish sunshine on each and every listen.

Sibelius: *Finlandia*

The unofficial Finnish national anthem was penned by Sibelius as a pro-Finland anti-Russia work, which made him hugely popular in his homeland for its nationalistic sentiments. It also ensured that his popularity grew across Europe too – but in other countries, it was the stirring melody rather than the composer's political viewpoint that sealed its place in every chart of the most popular classical works.

Mendelssohn: *Violin Concerto in E minor*

This is one of the greatest of all works for the violin, and mastering it seems to be a rite of passage for every promising young violinist, following a tradition set by the fourteen-year-old soloist Ferdinand David at the work's premiere in 1844. The second performance was given by another fourteen-year-old, Joseph Joachim, who would go on to become one of classical music's all-time violin greats.

Mozart: *Piano Concerto No. 21 in C*

He might have been twenty-nine years old when he wrote this piece, but it is worth remembering that Mozart already had twenty other piano concertos under his belt. He was the soloist in the premiere performance at the National Court Theatre in Vienna. You might sometimes hear this work referred to as the *'Elvira Madigan'*. This was because of its use in a now long-forgotten movie of the same name.

Mahler: *Symphony No. 5 in C sharp minor*

Although we think of him primarily as a composer today, it was as a conductor that Gustav Mahler was famous during his lifetime. He knew how to make orchestras sound powerful, with nearly all of his symphonies requiring a large number of players; they often last for over an hour each. His *Symphony No. 5* contains five movements rather than the usual four, including the achingly beautiful *Adagietto*, used in the 1971 film *Death in Venice*.

Beethoven: *Symphony No. 5 in C minor*

Surely the most famous opening two bars of any work in classical music, this symphony was premiered at the same concert in Vienna as his *'Pastoral' Symphony No. 6*. It must have been quite an occasion.

J. S. Bach: *Concerto in D minor for Two Violins*

Bach's Double Concerto for two violins was composed in 1717. A few years later, he created a new version for two harpsichords. When the original was lost, Bach scholars were able to reassemble the work based on the harpsichord transcription, so ensuring that it remains a firm favourite of the violin repertoire today.

Tchaikovsky: *1812 Overture*

Starting with a Russian hymn, featuring the French national anthem *'La Marseillaise'* along the way, with booming cannon fire and celebratory bells ringing out, this unashamedly triumphant and nationalistic work is one of the great showstoppers of classical music. Great performances don't just centre on the rousing final moments though; the best conductors perfectly contrast the delicacy of the earlier sections of the work, making the loud ending all the more effective.

Rimsky-Korsakov: *Scheherazade*

One of the most accomplished orchestral composers of all time, Rimsky-Korsakov taught many others how to master the art, including Prokofiev and Stravinsky. This suite, which is based on the tale of *The Thousand and One Nights*, was described by the composer as a 'kaleidoscope of fairy-tale images and designs of the oriental character'. The biggest musical hit of the four stories on which he concentrated is *'The Young Prince and the Young Princess'*.

Rachmaninov: *Piano Concerto No. 3 in D minor*

Not as famous as his *Piano Concerto No. 2*, this follow-up is fiendishly difficult for the solo pianist to play. In fact, the pianist for whom it was written, one Josef Hofmann, never actually performed it, apparently saying that the work was not right for him. In the right hands though, its expansive, rather grand style makes for a magnificent listen.

Tchaikovsky: *Piano Concerto No. 1 in B flat minor*

Around eighty years after this work was composed, it

became the world's first million-selling album after a recording was made by the pianist Van Cliburn. All three movements contain fabulous tunes, but they weren't initially to everybody's taste. When the composer played the concerto to the pianist Nicolai Rubinstein, Tchaikovsky was pointedly told that it was 'bad, trivial and vulgar'.

Beethoven: *Violin Concerto in D*

Given the amount of music that Beethoven composed, it seems surprising that he wrote only one concerto for the violin. Perhaps it was because it failed to gain popular approval quite as quickly as many of his other works. Things didn't start well for the work when the soloist at the premiere hadn't had time to learn his part and played most of it by sight – hardly what Beethoven would have wanted. There is, however, absolutely no doubt of the level of affection for the piece today.

About Classic FM

If this series of books has whetted your appetite to find out more, one of the best ways to discover what you like about classical music is to listen to Classic FM. We broadcast a huge breadth of classical music 24 hours a day across the UK on 100–102 FM, on DAB digital radio, online at ClassicFM. com, on Sky Channel 0106, on Virgin Media channel 922 and on FreeSat channel 721. You can also download the free Classic FM App, which will enable you to listen to Classic FM on your iPhone, iPod, iPad, Blackberry or Android device.

As well as being able to listen online, you will find a host of interactive features about classical music, composers and musicians on our website, ClassicFM.com. When we first turned on Classic FM's transmitters more than two decades ago, we changed the face of classical music radio in the UK for ever. Now, we are doing the same online.

The very best way to find out more about which pieces of classical music you like is by going out and hearing a live performance by one of our great British orchestras for yourself. There is simply no substitute for seeing the whites of the eyes of a talented soloist as he or she performs a masterpiece on stage only a few feet in front of you, alongside a range of hugely accomplished musicians playing together as one.

Classic FM has a series of partnerships with orchestras across the country: the Bournemouth Symphony Orchestra, the London Symphony Orchestra, the Orchestra of Opera North, the Philharmonia Orchestra, the Royal Liverpool Philharmonic Orchestra, the Royal Northern Sinfonia and the Royal Scottish National Orchestra. And don't forget the brilliant young musicians of the National Children's Orchestra of Great Britain and of the National Youth Orchestra of Great Britain. To see if any of these orchestras have a concert coming up near you, log onto our website at ClassicFM.com and click on the 'Concerts and

Events' section. It will also include many other classical concerts – both professional and amateur – that are taking place near where you live.

Happy listening!

About the Author

Darren Henley is managing director of Classic FM. His two independent government reviews into music and cultural education resulted in the creation of England's first National Plan for Music Education, new networks of Music Education Hubs and Heritage Schools, a new Museums and Schools programme, the new BFI Film Academy and the new National Youth Dance Company.

He chairs the government's Cultural Education Board and the Mayor of London's Music Education Advisory Group. A trustee of the ABRSM exam board, a commissioner the University of Warwick Commission on the Future of Cultural Value, and a vice president of the Canterbury Festival, he is the author of twenty-eight books.

Darren is a Fellow of the Royal Society of Arts,

the Radio Academy and the London College of Music; an Honorary Fellow of Canterbury Christ Church University, Trinity Laban Conservatoire of Music and Dance and Liverpool John Moores University; an Honorary Member of the Royal Northern College of Music and the Incorporated Society of Musicians; and a Companion of the Chartered Management Institute. He holds honorary doctorates from the University of Hull, Birmingham City University and Buckinghamshire New University.

Named 'Commercial Radio Programmer of the Year' in 2009 and the recipient of the Sir Charles Groves Prize for 'his outstanding contribution to British music', he was appointed an OBE in 2013 for services to music.

Index

Index

In the same series

The Classic FM Handy Guide to Classical Music
by Darren Henley

The Classic FM Handy Guide to Classical Recordings by Sam Jackson

The Classic FM Handy Guide to Ballet
by Tim Lihoreau

The Classic FM Handy Guide to Video Game Music
by Daniel Ross

The Classic FM Handy Guide to Film Music
by Rob Weinberg

The Classic FM Handy Guide to Opera
by Rob Weinberg